December 7, 1941

Letters from Hilltop House

"O'ahu has been attacked!"

Compiled by

Cosette Morrison Harms

DOCKSIDE SAILING PRESS®

Newport Beach, California

Newport Beach, California
www.docksidesailingpress.com
2

To the victims of December 7th, 1941

Hilltop House in the Early 1940s

Contents

Illustrations:

Foreword

Family and the Setting

Perched on top of the hill at Alala Point over-looking the communities of Kailua and Lanikai on the windward side of the island of Oʻahu, Hilltop House holds an unobstructed view of the ocean and across the bay to the Kaneohe Marine Corps Base Hawaiʻi on Mokapu Peninsula. Among the many historic stories associated with this landmark are those relating to its occupation as a lookout by the military during World War II. These letters written by **Anne Taft Powlison** at Hilltop during and just after the December 7, 1941 Japanese attack on Oʻahu give an inside look at what island residents were going through during those infamous days.

Anne "Nani" and Arthur "Skipper" Powlison with their three children, twins Peter and Peggy (9) and Jane (6), built their hilltop home in 1931. To preserve the beauty, strength and spirit of the rock formation on the hill, the house was carefully and lovingly constructed very much like a treehouse, tucked in and supported by these rocks in their natural form.

The next ten years were peaceful times. The children grew up playing on the pristine beaches below. Arthur, superintendent of Parks and Recreation, worked in Honolulu at City Hall. The children attended Hanahau'oli and Punahou Schools and were active in swimming competitions. The family also built a sailboat, the *Mokuola*, on which they enjoyed ocean adventures throughout the islands.

Sailboat *Mokuola* off Diamond Head

Saturday evening, December 6th, 1941, Arthur had taken friends out sailing off Honolulu on

Mokuola for sunset and full moonrise. Returning in the dark not far off Diamond Head and Waikiki he nearly lost control of the boat in large swirling whirlpools that tugged sharply on the tiller. He commented, "I wonder what Uncle Sam's submarine is doing out here tonight?" Moments later they noticed a fishing boat with no lights floating dead calm in the water. Its crew was frantically scurrying about on deck. Arthur sailed over and offered assistance. "No, Fine. Fine," was the nervous response. Puzzling over this encounter the crew of *Mokuola* returned to Ala Wai harbor with ominous feelings. Arthur stayed overnight in Honolulu with friends, as it was late when they came in and a long drive home to Kailua. The next day they realized they had probably interrupted a rendezvous between a Japanese submarine and fishing boat.

Hilltop House was full of family and weekend guests. Anne had cooked a large dinner for expected and unexpected visitors. Peggy (19), a civilian office worker at Pearl Harbor, had invited her date, architect Jim Morrison, for the weekend. Jane (16) was in high school and had been at a flying squadron dance at Schofield Army Base that Saturday night. She was a jitter bug champion! Her date, Army airplane mechanic Henry McMahon, drove her home and was convinced to spend the night rather than driving back across the island. Two photographers from Hickam Air Force Base had started a photo shoot of the house and decided to stay over. The only family not there besides Arthur was Peter (19), a student at the University of Washington, who was in Seattle.

Sunday, December 7, 1941

Fires from bombs dropped at Kaneohe (then called) Naval Air Station across the bay were the first signs to the breakfasting crowd that something was wrong. The military men and Jane took off in a car to investigate the "fires" only to return soon to report that the island was under attack by Japanese forces. Rushing back to their bases the three men found nothing but craters where they would have been had they not spent the night on the hill.

Arthur, being a friendly and playful guy had years ago painted a message on the tin roof of the house which said, ALOHA AIRMEN USA. From Kaneohe Naval Air Station pilots often flew low along the coast. The girls took pleasure in waving to

Hilltop House Welcomes U.S.A. Airmen

them when they came close, and the planes dipped their wings back and forth in response. It never occurred to them that this roof message would attract the attention of war planes on December 7th. The girls were outside and freshly hung laundry was flapping in the breeze. Suddenly airplanes appeared flying low and around Hilltop House. The insignia of the red circle of the rising sun was painted on their wings and bombs hung below. The planes, and others to follow, circled before heading toward Bellows Air Force Station just beyond Lanikai on the coast at Waimanalo. Perhaps it was the girls and the flapping laundry making Hilltop look like a residence that saved them from being bombed. The girls could hear the bombs being dropped at Bellows base.

For years afterward Anne recalled standing in a front window looking out during those terrifying moments when the Japanese low-flying bombers were circling the house. One plane flew so close and level with the window that her eyes met the eyes of the pilot. Fear rushed through her, the first fear of many in the years to come. By noon she was sitting with the girls in the upper room with its 360 degree view, watching and listening, terrified of invasion. There she wrote the first of many letters to her son Peter in Seattle. Her message: Be calm.

Like turning a page in a book—everything changed from peace to war. Anne wrote daily to Peter on tiny pages and mailed them every two to three days. Some were censored, returned and rewritten. They record the fears and preparations for the likelihood of invasion. They describe her observations of everything happening around her. She expresses so well her faith that keeps her strong and the heartaches and hardships of wartime Hawaiʻi.

As with all American families, big changes came fast after the attack. Arthur was consumed by his role with Oʻahu's Civil Defense and protecting the island from an expected invasion. Peter dealt with the pressure of leaving school to join the military. Peggy and Jim decided to get married sooner than later. Janie's school closed, only to re-open in a new location. Through all this turmoil was Anne's outward calm and reassurances. The last letter in this collection was written January 1, 1942.

So where have these letters been for 75 years? Only months ago, Peggy, now 94, and I, her daughter Cosette, were continuing our seemingly endless task of going through family memorabilia and photos. In a box labeled "to sort someday" we were amazed to discover this airmail envelope addressed to Peter having the postmark "Dec. 8, 1941." All of these treasured little pages were contained within that envelope and no one in our family remembered their existence.

Cosette Morrison Harms
Lanikai, Hawaiʻi, 2016

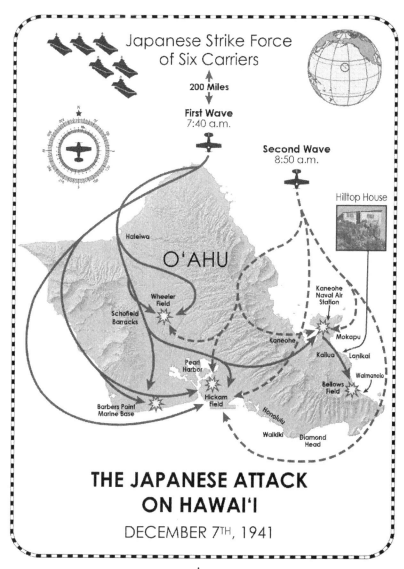

Japanese Strike Force of Six Carriers

200 Miles

First Wave
7:40 a.m.

Second Wave
8:50 a.m.

Hilltop House

Haleiwa

O'AHU

Wheeler Field

Kaneohe Naval Air Station

Schofield Barracks

Kaneohe

Mokapu

Kailua

Lanikai

Pearl Harbor

Bellows Field

Waimanalo

Barbers Point Marine Base

Hickam Field

Honolulu

Waikiki

Diamond Head

THE JAPANESE ATTACK ON HAWAI'I

DECEMBER 7TH, 1941

Sunday, Dec. 7, 1941

Beloved Pete,

It is 12 noon, dear heart, and I am on the big pūneʻe, and Peg and Janie are with me. I shall try to tell you of the horrors that we've lived through since 8:30 AM this morning. I'm sure you must have heard that Oʻahu has been attacked, and probably you heard it almost as soon as it happened. Doubtless you may have heard by now much more than we ourselves know for the radio is "blacked out," by order. Before it announced that it <u>was</u> going off the air, the Army Intelligence had ordered no one to use the telephone, and no one to use his car.

1

Sunday Dec. 7, 1941

Beloved Pete

It is 12 noon,
dear Heart, and
I am on the big
prunei and Peg
and Janie are with
me. I shall try to
tell you of the horrors
that we've lived there
since 8:30 Am this
morning. I'm sure
you must have
heard that Oahu
has been attacked
and probably you
heard it almost

2

"Keep your cars off the streets." "Keep all roads clear." "Drive your cars on the lawns if necessary, but keep them off the streets." "Stay inside your houses." "Keep calm!" "All major disaster officials report at once to your zones." "All ambulance units report to your headquarters." "All Senior University ROTC men report to the University of Hawaii for your equipment." "Inter Island announces that all sailing to and from Hilo and the other islands have been cancelled. Also all inter-island airplanes." These announcements were repeated again and again in English, Hawaiian, Chinese, Filipino, Korean, and Japanese. Now since twelve noon there has been only silence except for orders.

How a person like myself suffers to have those she loves where she can see and feel them! Arthur stayed in town last night and you are so far away! I shall try to put down in words what happened. Jim was here. Rodney Meyers and Dick High, both high up in photography at Hickam Field were here (to take pictures of the house for a mainland magazine). Also here was Henry McMahon, an airplane mechanic, whom Janie met at a flying squadron dance. We were all up and I was just starting to serve breakfast—warm homemade bread—when we suddenly discovered there was a huge fire at Kaneohe Air Base. We cogitated on the carelessness of people with matches and of cigarette smokers. It wasn't long before Janie and the three boys were in Henry's car headed for a close up look at the fire. None of us had the faintest conception that it had been bombed by a plane on which was the insignia of the rising sun!!! Jim and Pete Wilson had their day planned to work on their sailboat at Pearl Harbor and sail in races this after-noon. Peg was to join them towards sunset for a club dinner at the Yacht Club. Jim left and pretty soon the kids came back all excited at a report it was rumored that Pearl Harbor had been bombed and that Japanese planes had done it—and Kaneohe too. Well, the boys placed a call to Bellows and it was confirmed. They started gathering their gear to take off to get back to the Field when here right in front of us and above us and level with our windows were the fastest little planes you ever saw, and lo and behold the insignia of the Japanese flag on their wings. I thought we'd die of fright. Then there right before our eyes, bombs going down into the water almost to Kaneohe Bay with water rising hundreds of feet high. There was a thud of a great explosion and another big area went up in dense smoke at the aircraft area. And there before our eyes what we're sure was an airplane of ours, crashing into the ocean between here and Kaneohe. The boys left at once and we three girls have been alone throughout the day.

NAS Kaneohe Hanger #2 Burning

Now it is near sunset, Pete, and people have been afraid to stir or phone or anything. Military law was declared and Governor Poindexter made a stupid shaky dumb speech, and the order came through that the schools were closed until further notice and the school buildings were housing the evacuees from areas bombed. At long last Arthur got a brief phone call thru—said he had tried at various times during the day, but he could only be allowed a second and wanted to know if we were all right and to tell us he was at the City Hall—24 hour duty and all the hundreds on his committees were there working with him. He has been one of the high chairman heads of the disaster council ever since they organized months ago. Oh the strong comfort in hearing his voice!!! He will minister to the needful and scared. I wish we could hear your voice.

There will be trying days ahead of us. We may none of us know if or when airplanes or mail boats go. I want you to connect with us in spirit for a few moments as you waken, Dear, before you start the routine of your day, and again just before you go to sleep. Place each one of us trustfully and gratefully in the care of the one who is all Powerful and all

Wisdom and all Love. But don't stop there…. Surround the Islands with protection and that which they and all the people need, that right and health and normal happy living be established. But don't stop there either….Connect the whole haywire world with sanity and decent cooperative living. And then lift your heart into a calm, unworried place and keep it there, Pete darling!!! Believe full hearted in Right and Justice and a better order of things to come! Take each one of your moments throughout the day — one at a time as they come, applying yourself to normal, sane, <u>unworried</u> living, doing your best in your school work and in your swimming and getting all the weight and well-being you can out of every day! Accept and know we would want it to be that way. Get all that the blessed holiday time can bring you at Lyle's or wherever it is that you are Pete dear. Keep your letters coming as you can. I shall mail something to you every third day and will keep track of what I send. It is December 8th now and Janie and I are walking down to the Lanikai P.O. with this in a few minutes.

Peg went to work as usual and we have had no paper. We listened to President Roosevelt's speech this morning when he declared war. There have been two signal corps men in and out of our home all morning. Nice chaps, Irish and wholesome and clean. Had been on 24 hours and it eased my own heartache to feed them and have one take a nap in your room while the sergeant cleared lots of matters thru our phone. Found out quite a bit of inside dope: that they are "somewhere on this side," that there are quite a lot of Japanese snipers wearing blue jeans and the sun on their chest on this side of the Island, that the Clipper yesterday from the Coast landed at Hilo, that private cars and private homes below us have been shot at. But, Pete, we'll all keep our chins up and our Faith Undaunted and our Love Boundless in each other and in all things which are Good. And know always my Love and Faith and Pride in You now and Forevermore. God Bless thee and God Bless and keep us All.

I love you.

XOXOXO Your Mother Anne

Tuesday Dec 9th
My Precious Pete –
          Every day is
a year long and
every night is
longer than the day.
I'm sitting in
the toilet, – the
only spot in the
house where the
light can be on.
The girls are asleep
at last and I've
decided I'd like
it better in here
for a while. I'm
sitting on the
floor with my
back against
the door to the

9

Tuesday, Dec. 9th

My Precious Pete,

Every day is a year long and every night is longer than the day. I'm sitting in the little toilet room — the only spot in the house where the light can be on. The girls are asleep at last, and I've decided I'd like it better in here for a while. I am sitting on the floor with my back against the door to the girls' room and the edge of the shower is my desk. I've propped up your picture and it brings a certain nearness and comfort.

It seems inconceivable that on Saturday, three

days ago, life was normal, sane and serene!!! And now all outer things like navies, armies, governments, that from childhood on, you felt <u>could</u> protect you, well, you discover that your security cannot be placed in any of them, Pete, and that it has to stay only within <u>yourself</u>. There you can tune in with that which will never never fail you — Love, and Strength, and Peace, and Security. There you can know with certainty that <u>Life is</u> indestructible, that only the body that surrounds it and the material things that these bodies of ours can touch and feel can ever be destroyed. And Spirit will build again, and finally that which it builds will never be destroyed because what it builds is for the good of all — instead of selfish and greedy and possessive.

Peggy brought back word of Daddy. She was with him for several hours yesterday. He has a very responsible position in this disaster work and where people are jittery and so nervous they can't dial their phone numbers, he stays calm and reassuring. Peg stayed in town last night with the Mulders at the top of Wilhemina Rise. It didn't seem best that she make the drive over here, but things have become better organized today. Defense workers have permission to get a half tank of gas at a time, also the civilian defense people like Daddy. On his windshield is a big sign and he has to wear a white arm band with CD in red. His work has been holding him so late that he couldn't use the car to come home. All cars have to be off the road at nightfall and the few army autos, police cars or CD cars that go, have head lights and tail lights painted so dark blue that they barely crawl. The world looks so strange at night, accustomed as we are to the bright lights of the Kaneohe Air Station and the reassuring gleam of the Mokapu lights. Not a soul has a ray of light on in their houses. You can see if they even strike a match to light a cigarette, which by the way, has been proven that the flare of a match can be seen five miles and a glowing cigarette for three.

All liquor stores are closed. (The only good thing I know to come of all this horror!) Isn't it a commentary that our world should remember that when a national or local emergency like this happens, those in authority <u>close</u> the liquor shops because they know the miserable stuff unfits people for what they've got to do? All restaurants like Times, Kewalo etc. etc. where liquor has been available are closed also. All food stores are closed today and ordered to take inventory and make a report. It is expected that they will open tomorrow or soon with the order that homes may daily buy their customary amount at the store, only where they are accustomed to trade. Some will hoard and lay in a supply ahead, but I'm not going to. I'm going to live just one day at a time—conservatively, but not stingily, and I'm not going to be afraid to serve those who stray in at meal time besides our own. People are eating their meals at night about 4:00.

Peter and Anne

If it weren't that folks were so scared, they ought to get caught up on some much needed sleep. I should think that those who have scorned all things spiritual would go simply "cuckoo" now.

[Peter, from here on for two pages the letter which I wrote was censored. I'll lay it away just for fun so you can read them when life permits. The rest of this letter passed the censorship so it is being enclosed as written. I do hope my other letters have come thru to you. Only one of mine has been returned to me but by reports, the post office is very full of mail incoming and outgoing.]

Wednesday, Dec. 10th

Dearest Heart,

Well, here I am in the wee "writing room"! Janie and I both slept two hours this afternoon. Then we prepared a good supper: Irish and sweet potatoes, dried beef gravy, hot grape juice with lemon, Waldorf salad and cake that was baking during the Sunday attack. We had a dear family ceremony with this meal — all realizing and wondering when and if we'd have another one. Arthur got out here at about 4:15 and Peg came soon after. Darkness descended before we could get our plates back to the galley. Then we all made up the

15

big pūneʻe and talked and talked. Daddy hadn't realized what we had gone thru nor had we the faintest conception of the horror on the Honolulu side. Fire or ambulance sirens going without ceasing from Sunday morning when it began to the moment he came over today. He was the guest at the Mulders in Maunalani when it began Sunday morning, and they could not believe their eyes any more than we could here. Firing going on out in front and planes crashing etc. etc.

Pete, can you imagine trenches being dug around the library and sand bags piled up at all places to shoot behind? And our side with barb wire and trenches at Kailua Beach and gun nests all over the region? We try to get the mainland coast reports on our radio and if we can believe what we hear, then you're worried and blacked out and in a stew up there.

I must try and sleep now, dear heart. I do hope and pray that all is well with thee. Take each day as it comes and as we are doing, keep your chin up and keep faith. You are so so dear to us and our love surrounds you as I know your love is surrounding us.

XOXOXO Mother Anne

Kailua Bay

Thursday, Dec. 11th

Our very Dearest,

We are all home together again and exhaustion has claimed all but me. I feel wide awake as a hoot owl. I'm truly grateful that you didn't go to Wake or one of the Islands South. Their horror must be indescribable. We hear all kinds of reports and some of course are true. So many sending sets of radio seized and the people chucked into concentration camps. People whom Arthur and I both know are now dead.

Pete dear, by the paper tonight it means you

have to register—18-65 in age. With the irregularity and uncertainty of mail, all matters which you'd love to talk over with us will have to be decided by you. Turn within and pray, darling, asking that All Wisdom directs your every decision. <u>Listen</u> and <u>listen</u>, and follow your <u>inner hunches</u>, dear, for that inner hunch which you have is the voice of God directing you. It seems to Arthur and me that it might be best that you stay in school for as long as you can and get as much behind you as life will let you. But from this long distance, we can <u>not</u> advise on a single thing. Only God and you can make your decisions. If there is anything you need, send for it. Keep mailing your letters at least twice a week and we will too, <u>without fail</u>, and eventually mail <u>will</u> get thru, and by no break in its regularity, we can fit in the pieces and the pattern will tell the picture of what our days have held.

If your school days <u>have</u> to be postponed temporarily then try to combine with Lyle and Roland and boys you feel close to, and whose ideals are as yours and try and <u>stick together</u>! Remember defense projects will play their part in winning the war just as truly as carrying a gun, Pete. Do your part in keeping people around you from getting hysterical and going off half-cocked.

I will write more tomorrow and every day, and Janie will begin tomorrow too. She loves you full hearted as do all of us, ever and always. It does me good just to think of you. If this should be the last you receive by Christmas, Pete, know you will be there with us in our deepest thoughts and a candle will be in the window for you.

My Love XOXOXO Your mother Anne

PS. Your doctor said No blows on the head this year, dear. No water polo.
Please write common penny postcards to my sisters.

Friday, Dec. 12th

Dear dear Pete,

    Janie and I came into town with Arthur this morning with a list of things a mile long to get— staple things that if I'm not able to get into town for a while, the bare needs of life would be taken care of: thread, needles, these dear little pages of yours (I bought ten packages of them, Pete!!! I feel the dependence more than I ever have on the closeness I feel to you, and the elimination of miles that <u>while</u> I am writing comes over me.) I'm going to make out pages for you to fill in the answers in each letter I send now. And you do the same. There must be thousands of questions you'd like to have answered and the things you may be just paining to know, might never occur to us to mention. I shall try to anticipate as many of them as I can.

You'll be surprised when I tell you where I am. Janie and I are in line with a long procession waiting our turn to get our headlights "blacked out." They are painted a weird dark blue and spraying it on, the outside is darker than the very center. Punahou School you wouldn't recognize. It is the headquarters now of the U.S. Engineers. We haven't heard whether schools will open after January first or not.

I had not realized that a night letter to you of 25 words (16 message, 9 address and signature) was only $1.00 plus 10 cents tax. Let us both know, dear, that any extra important message from now on, you and we both can afford these night letters. Address yours thru Mackay Radio to Arthur Powlison, Lanikai, Kailua, Oʻahu. I just talked to the operator and he said that if he doesn't locate us here, he will put it on file to locate Arthur through the City Hall. On New Year's Day I hope you will send us a night letter starting us off on our 1942. They issue no information as to when and how mail will go to the Mainland from the Islands. There has come word however in the daily papers that all mail sent from here will be censored. It must not contain any statements which if read could be of any value if intercepted by an enemy. This letter will be the third letter which I have mailed to you since Sunday, Dec. 7th. I didn't know we weren't going to be allowed to write just as life is, and as we see and know it, so maybe you won't ever get to receive these letters, Pete. You know me, I write quite fully!!! I'll have to figure out another way.

My heart's love,
Mother Anne

Sunday, Dec. 14th

Dearest Pete,

It was so wonderful to be all together last night. Arthur came out with Peg and Jim and Jane and I had the banana wagon during the day. He had to be at a late meeting of the 2nd unit of the Civilian Coast Guard Reserve (He and *Mokuola* were in the first unit) so it was best that Janie and I make a dash for the hill. All civilian cars are off all the roads at nightfall. Our radios have brought us quite a bit of coast news and Seattle is sometimes mentioned. Once in a blue moon I get Seattle direct. Wish I always could.

At dawn Arthur went in to the City Hall to help with the tremendous undertaking of the gasoline allotment to car owners (10 gallons a month to private cars.) The line when he got there at seven reached clear to Beretania and up to Alapai (your barber shop street) and before the day finished the line was clear to Thomas Square. Jim has been helping me with blackout frames. Now the girls' room is very good. Permanent ones in the two windows on the bed and removable frames over the door window and the big window towards Kailua. When we sleep, we can lift them out and let the fresh air in. I shall fix the galley the same way with an adequate blanket over the stairs.

My love dear one. The girls and Daddy will be writing soon. This has knocked all speech out of them!!!

XOXOXO Your Mother Anne

Monday, Dec. 15th

Dearest One,

You'd think I'd have loads of time for letter writing but not so. Peg & I and usually Janie get up at 5:30 AM and I work right thru the day. This home is a center of peace & sanity and up building for so many many dear people. Back and around and below us are 24 hour watch and fortifications because of our location. The boys surely are appreciating us mightily. They're needful dear creatures and none of them are taking advantages. Then at any time of day and night our upper room is used by three high up officials in the Intelligence

Department—Wonderful people and it's a privilege to help. And I'm on call for Red Cross at Kailua Store and one of the committee members for fire prevention (sandbags and proper length attached hose). I walk down to the store once a day for the daily allotment and all in all, well, you've no idea how rushed the hours go by. The very thought of you helps me. You're strong and fine and loyal and splendid and I love you.

XOXOXO
Your Mother Anne

Just a note more before I mail this while I'm down at the store. We're all staying well and close and warm in our thoughts of you. I'm keeping a diary of more details than I show right now, which you'll get sometime. As I said in other mail, take your moments one at a time and expend no energies in worrying for worry just slays you, and does no good. Live just as normally and fully and happily as you can and we'll keep mail coming every three or four days and maybe you do too. I'm going to mail this now.

There are chuckles along with all the strangeness and darkness. Peg brought home a stick of licorice. You know we all <u>dote</u> on licorice—and announced that eating licorice was in keeping with the times! (blackout candy!!!) And she was so flustered one morning she put on two pairs of pants instead of one pair and wondered all day <u>why</u> she felt so <u>fat</u>! (As if an extra pair could fatten her up).

Will you give our special love to Roland, Don, Lyle, Marie, the Torneys, and Bob Buckley. All would have had letters from me at Christmas time but our thoughts will be with them and they will hear from us—when they hear from us. Our good wishes are nonetheless real and sincere though they may be unwritten just now.

God bless you dear and keep you ever,
Your Mother Anne.

Tuesday, Dec. 16th

Dear dear Son,

Until the censoring of mail is finished, I shall begin my letters this way, Pete, for it may save the censors time for other letters — knowing that the mother of a university student would have it also her responsibility that no injury could come to our nation and its individuals thru her.

We've been such good friends all these "nigh unto" twenty years that though I am always shamelessly proud that you _are_ my son and I am your mother, the usual role of mother does not come to

29

the front as in many mother-son relationships!

It is being not a little hard, but hard a <u>plenty</u> to receive no mail from you, Pete. The last we received was written Nov. 24 thru Dec. 1st and mailed by you on the 1st. This is my fourth letter since the 7th, when life changed with one "fell schwoop"! I feel as though that date were a century ago! (my other letters were mailed on the 9th, 12th, and 15th). I'm sure when you write you will let us know when letters start reaching you and which ones get thru. Our night letter was sent to you on Saturday, Dec. 13th, at least I think that was the day they said they thought it could get thru. You've never <u>seen</u> such lines of people to get their messages written, paid for, and then know that at least their radio was on the waiting list when messages became outgoing!

Jane is very cooperative. She had to have about two days and then she got herself on a splendid schedule. She spends between two to four hours each day typing. She has the red book and she is following it and is surely going to town. We get up at 5:30 AM when Peggy does, and we all eat a very hearty breakfast (or try to) and then I prepare a nice lunch for Peg. She lost weight and we decided to endeavor to get it back and add some if possible. So she takes a hearty sandwich, an apple, (a day, you know)! Some chocolate, some figs, celery, peanuts, cookies or cake, and she finds she is really eating it and enjoying it. It is quite late when she gets home and by the time supper is eaten and we've visited for a bit, she's so drowsy that she can hardly collect her wits and duds for the next day. With blackout still over Our Island and that added to the nervous strain, plus the labor of the day, we are sometimes asleep by seven or seven thirty. Peg is <u>very</u> <u>very</u> thoughtful and considerate and dear! She died hard on giving up the visit to you, leaving Feb. 13th. Of course all bookings are wiped out and they have asked that all who have paid deposits come in for them. When ships do begin again, they have asked the tourists to return to their homes (which of course makes sense) and the next group which are asked to go are the wives and children of the service personnel. In many cases that is very wise. We're hoping all of us whose roots have gone down and who prefer to cast our lot here will be allowed to but should that change, we'll descend upon you!!!! Jim is

Jane Powlison, Peggy Powlison, Ann and Arthur
Powlison, and Jim Morrison

nearly crazy with worry and sees no solution to his peace of mind except an immediate marriage to Peg. It is theirs to work out and I can see his side. A day at a time.

Going back to darling Janie: We put the house in perfect order (I mean sweep, dishes, etc. etc.) and do a little extra on that line every day. We've had to laugh about it, but that first awful day we couldn't eat; we couldn't seem to get out of the upper room! Had to watch and listen to the occasional directions issued by the radio. But we couldn't read either so I brought up the chamois skins and we washed the windows "the better to see you, ye blankety blank Blanks"!!!!!! Then I bought a lot of handwork (embroidery or gifts for Peggy) and Janie simply loves doing it and she does it beautifully. Then we wash clothes (in the sink!!!) and iron some every day. She is making a newspaper scrapbook beginning with Dec. 8th issues. It promises to be a classic. She is busy from morning to night. And I am busier than that! Joan Garvie and a lot of people are moaning and complaining that they have nothing to do. I can't get their point of view. I admit it must be hard on people who have been dependent on liquor (no sale since Dec. 7th), on playing cards, on the movies, and just anything that kept them from thinking. I hope that these days will teach them the riches in their own homes "acres of diamonds!"

Wartime Scrapbook

And dear dear dear Arthur! He does more good in one day than most people have accomplished in a lifetime! He is one of the few white men who detaches what some alien and American born "residents" have done from the honest prideful loyalty of others of the same race who will (and are) sacrificing and longing to serve our country. Arthur gives them confidence and courage and finds them tasks to do and their world becomes more stable and sane. He is working day and night on the major disaster recreation program of which he is the head. (He gets home with Mr. Roblee about 5 PM who has built the new house on the road back of us; they moved in about Thanksgiving time.) The foundational work is almost done and now they only need the "green light" to go ahead. I'm <u>so</u> proud of him.

More tomorrow dear dear one!
Your Mother Anne

Wednesday, Dec. 17th

Dearest Pete,

The days are <u>so</u> full and so unexpected. I wonder how much the papers there have carried of news from here. If it wouldn't be a bother I wish you'd slash out all the news and pictures pertaining to Hawaii and wrap a big envelope around it and mail it second class. It would reach us eventually and be <u>such</u> interesting reading. Often by tuning in on the coast stations we hear more than we get here— about ourselves. It's a strange world!

The three from the Intelligence Dept. stayed

here night before last and tonight Arthur Harris of the Police Dept. was here a long time. People in and out all day, observing, phoning, and getting information. One of the funniest calls was from Kaneohe headquarters to ask me to try and ascertain if there was anyone on top of the telephone pole mauka of us who was signaling with flashlights—that it had been reported twice. It had been raining and you know how the electricity dances between the red balls in that maze of wires. I <u>knew</u> it was that, but I went and looked and of course it was. Arthur saw a white flare straight out to sea at 6:30 tonight which we did report because we didn't like it. Art Harris swapped lots of news: that the Japanese population moved out of Aiea Saturday night. They <u>knew</u>. Your hair would stand on end at some of the things we hear. And Pete, you know where you went to have your ankles treated near the streetcar barns? He operated a carrier pigeon service to the enemy via sampans. He is now in the concentration camp.

I feel very weary since the walk to the store. Shall try to snatch a bit of sleep.

Oh to <u>hear</u> from you! I do hope all is well with

you. God bless you and keep you.

XO Your Mother Anne

Hilltop House from Kailua Bay

Thursday, Dec. 18th

Oh Pete! This should be in red ink only because it is a Red Letter day of deep satisfaction!!! Your blessed letter got through and Arthur brought it home with him. He had been so rushed he hadn't opened it so we all got in a huddle on the big pūne‘e and we're <u>so</u> happy. They were the pages from Dec. 1st thru the 7th. Then I served a good supper and they all ate and ate and then we all got down in the girls' room and talked and talked and talked. Daddy was full of his experiences and plans and Peg was of hers and by 7:30, Arthur and I turned in and went to sleep. By one we were as awake as hoot owls and he put the radio on and it was Hawaiian music—probably for the tiny brave island south of us—no announcements or titles to songs just beautiful beautiful music. I fixed us hot Ovaltine and we discussed pros and cons of the three big CD (civilian defense) centers he hopes to open in tents and he jotted down ideas in the dark. Now he is back to sleep and I'm in the girls room with my back to the telephone and it is three-thirty. I want this mailed in the morning, though I have no idea when mail will go from here or if any has gone as yet. I went to sleep with your letter under my pillow where my hand could touch it. Shall reread it now and answer the high spots.

I know your course this quarter has simply been a <u>killer</u> and with the situation for living and beginning your year so so difficult when it comes to giving your Best to studying—well all I can say is that I pray daily that you <u>will pass</u> with a margin that will let you swim but if you don't—well, you will receive no censor here—just love and understanding. Oh Pete, that <u>is</u> so SWELL and such accomplishment to be the best man at Doris' wedding! I'm truly tickled pink and proud as anything!!! Will your dark blue suit be suitable to wear? Be sure you have <u>good</u> new black shoes which do not <u>squeak</u>! It would be disastrous if they did you know. And do describe it all in greatest of details.

Your letter was mailed on the 8th; today is the 18th. It made very good time considering and it was not opened by censor. Put Univ. of Wash. under your name on the return address between it and your street address and maybe none of your letters will be opened. Also "Powlison Family."

Now as to what we <u>truly</u> want you to do, Pete dear, it is to stay in school for as long as you can for it is maybe now or never to get your preparation for your life work. When war was declared and radio and papers here had it 18 to 65 for draft and the orders to enlist at once etc. etc. — plus the threats we heard to the safety of the whole west coast — I lived through the tortures of the damned wondering what you might or would be forced to do, as well as perhaps get snarled up in a frenzy of mass action. We did <u>not</u> want that to happen nor do we now. It looks now as though selective service is urged instead of volunteers which is truly right and the only way we hope and pray that it is 21 to 45 which does permit youth to get life preparation farther along. For that is the only way, Pete, there can be leaders and life goes forward with sanity. I feel <u>so</u> comforted to get your letter and it gives me hope that letters can keep getting thru—ours to you and yours to us.

In my first one I told you what I shall repeat lest it never reached you. Live as normally and sanely as possible getting all you can from the Christmas holidays and from every day as you possibly can. And give forth sanity, tolerance, faith, confidence to all around you there. That is being truly a Good American. I think I can catch a nap now and oh Pete, how we do all love you! You are our pride and joy. You'll smile at my involved address on my other letters. I had no idea when it might get thru to Seattle or what the situation might be up there so I did all I could think of to help it get thru to you. I don't know when the others will connect with pen and paper but they truly love you!!!

A candle will be in the window for you Christmas Eve and our thoughts and love.

XOXOXO Mother Anne

The Friendship Candle

Friday, Dec. 19th

My dear dear Son,

Pete dear, my letter to you with pages of days Dec. 9 thru Dec. 11 has been returned with pages 6 and 7 marked with a "40" and a "47." Inside was a form—a slip of paper stating, "This letter is returned to sender for revision because it contains information not verified or is considered harmful to national defense. Please rewrite and mail again. Information Control Branch."

I feel so chagrined and it was the last thing I'd

have done knowingly. I have finished my sentence on a new page 6, and omitted page 7, and as they suggested, am sending on to you the rest of the letter. We are all well and today is such a tired day, I'll write more tomorrow.

My love full measure.
Mother Anne

Pete, Arthur says kindly lay off water polo. It is as dangerous as football. Blows to the head and kidneys are dangerous.

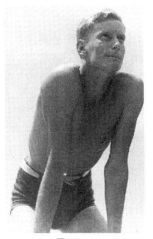

Peter

Saturday, Dec. 20th

Dear dear Son Pete,

   I've spent the day in town—the 2nd day I've had there since Dec. 7th. Janie & I made the first installment of Christmas bread yesterday and today I delivered to Christine Thompson, Margaret Smith, Cosette Mulder, the Irving Johnsons, Verna Mayfield and the Meisners. Three out of the six had never had my bread for Christmas, but they had eaten it, and loved it, and knew how we felt about it. They as well as the others felt so deeply about it when I brought it to them that it has left me feeling warm all over and sort of singing inside. Something about it seemed so real in an unreal world, and so sane and understandable in a crazy realm, sort of like a strong hand to cling to!!! To the Meisners, Christine and Margaret it was a bit of life-as-it-used-to-be, that they loved and understood!

I bought a very few things—all necessaries—and a bill book just like I sent you for Daddy. (I mean Peg did, but that one of Thackers I exchanged for the one in your Christmas box as it had zippers in the right spots.) Daddy has so many cards now, he wants one. Oh Pete dear I <u>hope</u> your Christmas box got to you. It was mailed the day before the Lurline's last voyage, and the Lurline reached the Coast in safety on Dec. 10th by verified reports. By your letters I believe you had also mailed packages to Daddy & Janie & Peg and we will tell you when they come.

No changes here. Everybody sitting tight.

My prayers & Love,
Mother Anne

Sunday, Dec. 21st

Very Dearest Pete,

Daddy's work doesn't let him come back last night or tonight. He is doing a splendid piece of work. About three hundred under him now. We're all very proud of him. I had to howl at something he said with so much mischief—that Frank Atherton's card which permits him to be on the streets at night had to be signed by Arthur!!! Many other "big shots" also!!! The community is really grateful for Arthur and they are listening to what he says. All day long we three girls have been busy busy busy making the living room look Christmassy. It makes a bit of stable reality and a lift of heart for not just us but these many many fine fellows who are surrounding us and on duty day & night. One of them produced a dear little tree—from where we'll never know!!! The Christmas tree ship didn't get thru and, well—"only God can made a tree" you know. It was going to be our first Christmas without one and we prepared the room accordingly—the shrine on the little low table near the marimba, and Island holly in bowls, and on my little bureau that little artificial tree that Christine brought to *Mokuola* while she was being built under the trees; it looks lovely atop deep blue paper with make believe snow; then over on the radio we put more dark blue paper with that silver star tree that has always been on Janie's shelf; above that and pasted to the window are the lovely arches that look like a stained glass window in a church. It is <u>beautiful</u> there and in the window above dawn corner we fixed the same shade blue paper in panel with that white "Merry Christmas" thumbed tacked on and lovely stars pasted here & there. Over the window going down to the galley is a wreath. Of course in your window is a dear green candle for you. And now there is the **<u>tree</u>**! A dear little Norfolk Island pine (you know those dark stiff green ones) and it is on the rock table in the center. We are the only Christmas all these boys are going to have, Pete, and we're proud to be a home they simply <u>love</u>!

So sleepy now. God bless thee and keep thee safe. We all love you so.

XOXOXO Mother Anne

Monday, Dec. 22nd

Dearest Pete,

Janie fell down the galley steps last night tripping over the flour can on the steps forgetting it was there from making bread. So, she had to go to Dr. Clark's today. Her right wrist is in a splint but I guess aside from that she will not be laid up too much. Arthur & the girls are asleep but I want this to go tomorrow **surely**. Oh Pete, dear one, today two letters got thru from you! One was mailed Dec. 10 with pages December 8th and 9th, and the other was mailed on Dec. 18th with pages December 15 thru the 18th. That means we've missed one letter but

51

here's hoping and praying it shows up. I will repeat once more when I've mailed letters to you: On Dec. 9th, pages 7th–9th; on Dec. 12th, days 9th–11th (this was returned & is now enclosed); on Dec. 15, days 12th–15th; on Dec. 19th, days 15th–18th; and now, on the 23rd, days 19th–22nd.

Now for brief comment on your letters, darling. I can put myself in your place and know how ghastly it must be to be so far away and not be able to know all you'd like to know. It would be most comforting to have you here, you know that, but as I have said in letters you doubtless have not received as yet, Arthur and I truly desire that you get as much of your college completed as is humanly possible. The world will need leaders and trained people to bring order and stability and cooperative living when right living is allowed to triumph again. You will have to register when the orders come for selected service which fits your age, and I will get to you the credentials of your birth in my next letter. There's no news, which I dare to record, darling. Your papers there doubtless tell you more than we'd be allowed to write.

Must sleep now. More tomorrow and always. my prayers and deepest love.

XOXOXO Mother Anne

We do hope you are going on with your vacation plans and living normally and with your old sweet dear enthusiasm. Do hope your Christmas Eve and Day are blessed in every way, also that nothing has interrupted your days with Don and Margo. We must all keep sane and serene and keep life full and rich for all those around us. That will help win the war. Sweet Sleep.

Tuesday, Dec. 23rd

Dearest Son Peter,

I sent you a letter yesterday—no I mean this morning—with days 19th-22nd. That was the fifth letter I have mailed since the 7th. I do hope my mail is reaching you. I have felt so very depleted in energy today that I have not accomplished much. Janie and I have been making Bread. We always in spirit send you some of every batch. I have heard from all my sisters and they feel anxious about us. Buy a few 1¢ post cards & occasionally send one to them. Do not take time for letters. It is not necessary. I don't know if I made my postscripts clear. Arthur

54

feels if it isn't <u>necessary</u> to play water polo, it is much better not to, as, so many kidneys are injured etc. and Dr. Cushnie hoped there would be no blows on your head for at least a year. Pete, always please tell us just how you feel physically. We keep nothing from you and pray that you never will from us.

We love you with our full full hearts.

XOXOXO Your Mother Anne

Wednesday, Dec. 24ᵗʰ
Christmas Eve

My very Dear One,

Your spirit has been very very close and near and comforting. The rest are fast asleep but I wanted a few moments with you before I went shut-eye. Janie and I got the house so lovely. Jim brought us two lovely poinsettias and the Playground Assn. a beautiful wreath (in the door as usual) and we had waffles just as always, and tuna gravy and cabbage salad (the cabbage cost 45¢ instead of 10¢!!!) and Christmas carols and Dickens story (Tiny Tim's "God bless us every one") and news on the radio all

56

evening long. The stars and the night was lovely and peaceful and I'm grateful!!!

Jim gave Peg her beautiful beautiful beautiful engagement ring and I announced it with cute little cards. He is truly a dear sweet person. He wants to take such good care of us all, Pete, not just of Peggy and in these troubled times that is most comforting and sustaining. Do know that you <u>are</u> helping us by being right where you are. No ship could bring you for the time being. (We hear the Islanders longing to get back can't be given any assurance until February.)

The movement of forces probably will be to the west but no one knows. My heart feels for the mothers with sons in the Philippines. Oh our troubled world — and its fates guided by such a few instead of the masses of "just folks" whose natures would so prefer to live and let live. God help us all and let's try to put our Faith in Him and in the eternal Rightness of things to come. And so I bless you and across the miles my arms do hold you tight and I feel the dear comfort of you — strong like a Rock, and Dear and Fine. God bless thee and keep thee, now and ever.

My devoted Love,
Mother Anne

'Iwa in Flight

Thursday, Dec. 25th
Christmas night 11:30 PM

Dearest dear Pete,

All the rest of us are asleep—ten of us under the roof tonight and last night: Jim, Inez Brewton, Paula Emery, Marjorie Stone, David Thompson, Hawley Marion and your four own. So many many many people would like to have been with us but long hours of duty and blackout hours intervened.

I'll start with today when we wakened at about 6:30 AM. Many 'iwa birds were gliding thru the air and Dawn was so so lovely. Arthur had to leave at eight so we all gathered on the big punc'e around him and we opened the packages. I bought him slippers—he had had none since Hill School days—and Peg bought him a blue sport shirt, and Janie the traditional razor blades, and shaving cream. To it she added a comb in a case for his pocket (and on her card she wrote, "I hope this can always comb thru something"!!!) and a nail file for his pocket with "your own"—for he just never can find a nail file! And I bought him a pocket book just like yours for he has so many cards and passes now. He was so pleased. And <u>of course</u> there was the traditional old green <u>can</u> that he gets <u>every</u> year. It paid to keep Christmas just as much like it has always been and its strength and comfort will always abide with us. Peg is buying us a second-hand electric refrigerator. We haven't had ice since the 7th. Bless her. And she bought me a house coat and I'm thinking of that as from you both. One arm a piece! XO And I bought for them both a few doodads like a 10¢ 1942 diary, and little necessary gadgets. Peg did the same for Janie. It was all very sweet and dear. And your spirit was close and warm.

After breakfast was stowed away there was the great urge to go for a sun and a swim. Everyone is getting sure nuf "white meat" and since the 7th there hasn't been a soul on the beach for a swim or a sun. They all look so healthy tonight. The day was beautiful and they all got a good pink color.

I had a "chore" which simply had to be done. A terrific odor issued forth from the corner where you step up to get on the girls bed. A trap had been snapped a few nights ago and the huge creature had crawled behind the inner black chest of drawers which you can't budge or just do anything about. Where there is a will there is a way and at the end of three hours of trying to collapse into smaller dimensions in some spots and longer ones in others, I got the horrible Pest out and the spot lysoled and flitted. As for myself, I didn't know whether I should be buried or boiled to feel clean again. I decided on a half hour's scrubbing in the shower and ended up with talcum, toilet water and the new house coat and felt like a human being, though a very weary one, for the rest of the day. Imagine an ordeal like this on Christmas Day when I wanted to feel spiritual as well as gay!!!! By the time I had gotten myself horizontal on the big pūne‘e they strolled up from their swim and I just lay there and announced that I was hungry and the getting of lunch was up to them. They did!!!

But the day was dear, Pete, lots of the service boys strolled in and ate my bread, cupcakes and cookies and peanuts and candy. They truly truly appreciate our Home and some of them call me Mom with such affection. Arthur got back at 5 PM and dinner was completely ready. Peg had bought three little chickens which I had stuffed and roasted & made buckets of the yummiest of gravy. Then there were mashed potatoes—so so good—home-made cranberry jam and celery and a coconut cake that was given to us and a fruit & nut plate. We all ate until we could hold no more and Hawley & Jim did the dishes. Daddy was wound up and talked & talked and talked and at ten fifteen they were all in bed. I found I was as wide awake as a hoot owl so I'm here writing at the kitchen sink.

Peg and Jim went down and sent you and his parents a night letter. I think their decision to marry New Year's Eve is doubtless wise. They both feel so enthusiastic about it and folks should marry when they truly want to if they can afford it. And Jim wants that the place they get is large enough for us all to sleep in town and that we all are there whenever it is best, and that they are here the same. It will work out so much better for Arthur when he has to stay in, and they do want to take good care of Daddy. The opening of the big tent at Beretania and the Civic Auditorium was a big success today. Bless him. So many victories as the days do hold for him.

It looks now as though there will be just Arthur, Janie, Jackson Hawkes & Dick Gunn here when the ceremony is performed. Jackson to perform the ceremony and it will depend on the weather whether it is indoors or outdoors and at sunset or by moonlight. We'll all long and long for you to be here Pete, but we will be hoping that you are with Don and making them very very happy there, darling. In that way, you make us happy here too.

Now I am sleepy at long last and I will sign off so this can be mailed in the morning. Your sweet loving spirit is very helpfully to us. Rest and prepare for the opening of school and live one day at a time with great faith and confidence that Right will triumph.

I love you.

XOXOXO Your Mother Anne

Friday, Dec. 26th

Very dearest Peter,

I've talked with Daddy about your return to Hawaii at this time. He feels that it is for you to stay in school for as long as you can and get all it has for you for Life's preparation. That is what he thinks best. But when it comes to selective service register your residency here & permanent home as here will let your number be called from here (if that is your pleasure) so we might all see you before you go into active service.

These are times when it would mean oh so

much to be able to afford an occasional long distance phone call! Thank all the good powers that be, we are able to write to each other every day. I shall always mention the dates I have sent forth your letters since the seventh, and you do likewise. Two of yours have come thru as yet — the ones mailed on the 8th and the 18th. Also your individual Christmas cards mailed on the 11th. Marie's powder case to Peg has come thru but not your packages as yet. We do hope our package which was sent in time to go on the Lurline which left here Dec. the 5th reached you. My letters to date are as follows:

Days of Dec. 7-9th

Dec. 9th–10th mailed the 12th

Dec. 12th–15th mailed the 15th

Dec. 15th–18th mailed the 19th

Dec. 19th–22nd mailed the 23rd

Dec. 23rd–25th mailed the 26th

The hectic grind for Arthur continues to keep up but he has the great satisfaction of knowing that he is accomplishing much. He combines with Judd Roblee in the new house below us to use only the one car to go back and forth. Tonight he is on all night duty as member of the Coast Guard Unit One

Auxiliary. God bless him. The girls and I have had one of our precious sweet times, puttering around and hearing the Kraft Hall of the Air, but sleep claims us almost as soon as darkness falls. Our adjustable blackout frames permit fresh air except for the few minutes they are in and the flood of light and beauty when they are not in. Can you picture our world with total darkness—6 PM to 6 AM these 20 nights? Some people chaff under it but we haven't, nor has no sale of liquor changed the even tenor of our ways.

I shall go in tomorrow to help Peg with her shopping. They (Jim & Peg) sent you a night letter yesterday.

Sweet sleep now and God Bless,
Mother Anne

Saturday, Dec. 27th

Dearest dear Pete,

You know me when I go to town! I'm geared only to the country. Too too sleepy I am to scrawl even a page. Arthur beat Jim, Peg & me home tonight. All's well with Daddy—just heavy with sleep, and now with a good supper in his tummy. He always says, "This is the best meal since my last one here!" It has always been my pleasure and privilege to do things for Arthur and take good care of him. I know people think I spoil him and also you Three, but I'd rather be too good to people, than not good enough, and I think you're all turning out a credit to the Taft-Powlison ancestors so folks shouldn't squawk. Night now Beloved One and a prayer.

XOXOXO Your devoted Mother

Altar Rock

Sunday, Dec. 28th

Dearest Dear,

The rest are all asleep but I desire these moments with thee before I do. The moonlight is simply incredible and its transforming power! The search lights to the left of us focusing in a high prolonged beacon have made a path of reflected light across the water as though a full moon there was vying with God's real one. Such a Hilltop for seeing things! Never more so Pete, and we'll tell you all, the moment we can! We want no censored mail from our family. It wouldn't fit in with what we're all doing to help set the rising sun and Hitler!

Again we all went to town today. Arthur busy from morning to night (his week is at least eight days long!) Janie visiting in one of the boy's home (stationed on the hilltop behind us & he is having his first leave!) and Jim & Peg & I house hunting for them. They have decided on one at 2655 Waolani Ave. (This street begins at the extreme end of Wylie — turn right as Wylie finishes and it is the last house on the right.) They have bought all the furniture as is, even to sheets and towels and dishes & cooking utensils from a very lovely navy wife and children leaving for the coast. The house isn't new but it has the old charm of space (even a little dining room) and located as it is, Jim & Peg will avoid the city traffic getting to work.

From 1:30 to 4:00 we were at KGU with a fine representative group of the Cruising Club, the first meeting since Dec. 7th. Isn't it remarkable and truly a credit to the officers, especially to AKP & wife!!! that since the idea of the club was born on Dec. 12, 1938 there has never been a month without a bulletin, and always there has been at least one gathering!!! Irving Johnson is going to be a presenter. He speaks so slowly and with such sincerity with his two feet and body firmly on the ground.

We must get a letter from you soon. So so hungry for the sight of your handwriting. Sweet sleep now and more tomorrow. I love you full hearted and truly I have great confidence in the days ahead for us all.

XO Your Mother Anne

Monday, Dec. 29th

Dearest dear — or rather I should say good morning, Pete, as it is three thirty in the morning. The north wind howled and the rain began and sleep fled, so here I am.

I spent Monday in town and helped Arthur the whole day thru — 7:00 to 4:30. Then we rode out with Jim and Peg in Jim's car. They had to pick up their license at Kaneohe on the way out as Arthur checked on his three workers there. (I just heard a rooster crow. It sounded so sane and homey and good!!!) Arthur needed me to secure hostesses for his new CD centers and I think I'll have to go in for the same tomorrow.

We all got up on the bed in the girls' room and worked on our original announcement. Such good laughs. Arthur and Jim get such a kick out of each other and of course they periodically howl at me. I'll write you in complete detail about every-thing. You know how we long for you to be here with us, darling, yet so sure we are that you nor we will ever regret that you have these days of pre-paration right where you are. Truly serving is also a thing of the spirit, too, you know, and you can be a well of strength, clear thinking (allow no hate of human beings—just of some of the things which they do!!!) and perspective, putting first things first and keeping the long look ahead—not the close range which can blot out more than it can ever see. It will be a temptation to let studies slide & go hay wire. To not do so takes character but you have it and can inspire others to have it. We love you so! More tomorrow and deepest love from Arthur, Jane & Peg were they awake. God bless thee, ever and always.

XO Your devoted Mother, Anne

Tuesday, Dec. 30th

My Dearest Son, Pete,

I mailed you a letter when I was in Honolulu today with the days from Dec. 26th thru the 29th. Since the 7th I have mailed you letters on the 9th, 12th, 15th, 19th, 23rd and 26th. When mail can reach us and ours you as normally, check up on the ones you've sent and the ones which you have received. The last we received from you were those written on the blue paper to us individually dated Dec. 11th. Seems eons ago.

Much is happening in Arthur's work. It was

necessary that I go in and lend a hand these last two days. I accomplished much these past two days. The women volunteer workers are shaping up fine. All who work in these "Civilian Defense" (CD) centers wear arm bands with the V...and our heads are humming. Daddy appreciates me and I do him & we <u>Love You.</u>

Mother Anne

Wednesday, New Year's Eve - 1941

My very very dear One,

All are asleep and though it is well past the midnight hour, I feel sleep will come sooner to me if I write awhile to you. You have been in our most loving thoughts throughout the preparation for Peg's wedding. With Arthur needing me, it hasn't let me prepare for it as I should have liked to, but the essentials always seem eventually to get done! Janie and I made bread and the old standby devil's food cake. On the cake we wrote Peg and Jim in white candies, and put the little figures of the boy & girl in wedding costume in between the names. And

I bought the biggest ripe olives I could find, and for Christmas, we were given macadamia nuts, and I made a huge platter with lettuce, tomatoes & avocado (no celery to be had) and, oh yes, we had potato chips and candy kisses. It gets dark very early so almost as soon as Arthur, Jim and the two Elders (Jackson Hawkes and Dick Gunn) arrived (near five) we brought the food.

I bought a most expensive ($1.50) white candle. It is about 18" to 24" high and wide at the base, tapering just enough to be graceful. But the charm of it is, it's almost transparent (color of snow whiteness) plus the fact that it has the appearance of solid candle drippings all over its surface. It is heavenly beautiful. Peg & Jim lighted it a few minutes before six, when Arthur & I lighted the one on the rock, and Janie your dear green one in the window by the Pi'ikoi rock. You were very very near & dear! Peg & Jim's candle will be put away until next New Year's Eve and always burned for a while on each anniversary. There were three bowls of deep dark red roses. On the card table was a lunch cloth & napkins (paper) with sailboats (couldn't find any wedding figures) blended with two bowls of roses, the candle, the cake & the dishes of nuts and kisses. It was really lovely. The upper room was truly lovely.

Peg was ravishingly <u>beautiful</u>. Her hair is quite long and she keeps it so clean and lovely. Jim bought her a large white orchid and a <u>long</u> full white carnation lei. You must wear "something <u>old</u>" (her white shoes when she graduated from High School), "something <u>new</u>" (a heavenly holoku of a wonderful red with lovely white night blooming cereus splashed all over it.) It was the prettiest holoku I've ever seen and most flattering and becoming! Let's see: "something old and something new;" "Something <u>borrowed</u>" (Janie's little four leaf clover pin. When Arthur & I married I picked a <u>real</u> four leaf clover as I neared the canoe.) "Something <u>blue</u>." (Of course you'd know that would be a blue bead. We slipped it on to one of the strands of the silver ribbon on her lei.) Janie wore her holoku and Jim brought her a pink carnation lei and an orchid for her hair. I wore a borrowed light blue holoku & a red carnation lei with red roses for my hair. Arthur was in his sport blue shirt & his blue coat & pants, and he & Jim had a white carnation in their coat lapel. Jim wore a white suit. He is a dear dear sweet person Pete, and I believe he & Peg are in for a comfortable happy married life.

Peggy's Wedding Day

They asked that nice Jackson Hawkes (the Mormon elder) to perform the ceremony. Our good friend, Elder Dick Gunn was with him and they made the nicest ceremony <u>ever</u>. I had written one page regarding the symbolism of our Hill for a marriage ceremony and Dick read that as the service began. Then after the service was over, Dick read us (by moonlight) an original poem which he had written about it all. We will mail you these in our next letter. I think you'll like them. Peg & Jim stood facing the ocean in front of the Altar Rock. Peg walked out with Arthur from the front door and on the little portable radio, that lovely Hawaiian song "Makalapua" was being played out by the rock. The night was one of those snow white, transfiguring moonlight evenings — billowy clouds, all the varying depths of coral and ocean in color, and the mountains all mystery and nearness. (No mosquitoes either, thank goodness.) It was all so natural and sweet and yet dignified. Afterward we (only 7) all stood in a huddle with our arms around each other like a football team and Arthur reminisced about our ceremony and then we went in by and by and danced. We all spoke of you **so** many times. It was 12 midnight where you were when their ceremony

81

began, or was it!!? You know Arithmetic and me, Pete!!!

I do hope Don's plans went on as originally planned! So many things I hope!!! That you are well!!! That the year 1942 is a <u>good</u> year for you, and happy, victorious and full of that which you value. Broken up into minutes or perhaps at times into seconds, no moment will prove to be too much for any of us. When our strength leaves off, our Great Invisible Partner's will never fail us. This occasion, Peg's wedding, warranted a better recital than I've given but it will enable you to see it a bit. It's to try and sleep now Dear Heart. Your strong arms would feel powerful good to me this second!!!! Time out, to indulge in a good old fashioned weep! My first today—and for a long time. Pau now!!!

Love, full measure,

XOXOXOXOXO Mother Anne

New Year's Day
Thursday, Jan. 1st, 1942

My dearest Pete,

It is night now and all the rest are asleep. The day has passed quietly — as a Sunday — but busy for us. Janie held down the Hill and Arthur, Jim & Peg and I went in this morning returning at six tonight. It was a busy day at the centers. 1500 or more at the New Year's dance 1 to 4 PM this afternoon at Civic Auditorium. The only New Year's dance held — unique in Honolulu's history.

Peg & Jim & I worked on their moving & settling. Jim got his stuff all over from where he lived and we "toted" up the stuff from Chadwick's—bed, bureau, trunk, pictures, etc. etc. They have taken a house at 2655 Waolani Ave. which is at the end of the last street when you get to the end of Wiley & turn right. With mail so hard to get thru I hope you'll continue addressing as before—to the family at Room 601 City Hall, and we'll see that she gets it too as soon as possible. Arthur will be sleeping there when it serves his needs, as will we all. Your wire hasn't been read by us yet, but Bill Chadwick told me he took it out of the ether between midnight & dawn and we're looking forward to reading it. XO! We'll use night letters ($1.10) whenever anything warrants from now on, Pete, and let's make it always via Mackay as its station near here receives it & we'll get it sooner. More <u>very</u> soon.

God bless you and keep you.

XO Your one and only Mom

Epilogue

As described in Anne's letters to Peter, Hilltop House became a hub of military activity immediately after December 7th. Anne was compassionate and inclusive preparing meals for whoever was there. Invasion was still expected and tension was high. The family came and went from school and work until eventually, on April 1, 1942, the U.S. Army determined the need to occupy Hilltop House full time as a lookout and gun control center. The family was paid $30 per month "rent."

U.S. Army Occupies Hilltop House

The guns were mounted in the foothills behind Kailua and Lanikai. Concrete pillbox-shaped lookouts were hidden on the ridges. Around-the-clock shifts were kept and a chow wagon delivered their meals from the air base.

Anne, Arthur and Jane moved in with newly married Peggy and Jim Morrison in Honolulu. Cosette was born to them in 1943. The family then rented a larger house on Ehukai St. in Waimanalo. Here they opened their home and hearts to countless servicemen and women to come find R&R and family time. Never knowing how many people would be there at mealtimes, Anne became highly skilled in stretching the food to fit the crowd— sometimes watering down the black bean soup to fill the bowls. There were only two "house rules" for their military friends: wear aloha attire and be known only by first names. Here they found a rare respite from rank and military protocol.

Jane continued to create scrapbooks of war-related newspaper clippings. She graduated in '43 from Punahou School's war campus located at the University of Hawai'i.

Peter left the University of Washington, enlisting in the U.S. Marines in 1942, and served in the Pacific throughout the war.

Gratefully Hilltop House was returned in

perfect condition to the family on April 1, 1945. Anne had left a guest book with the story of the family and the house. The men who were stationed there filled its blank pages with their thoughts and sentiments.

To quote from a few:

"You folks who built this house left more than a frame building when you turned over Puuhonua to us. You superimposed your love of the sea, the mountains and the rocks, and a spiritual welcome awaited us as we entered its doors."

"This house is not just a house. Instead it is a shrine that typifies exactly what we are fighting for in this war."

"Today, the first of the gangster nations has surrendered (Italy) and who knows what tomorrow will bring? One thing certain, one of these tomorrows, we will be able to return to our 'houses of refuge' and you to yours. In the meantime we are grateful for yours."

"When I leave the little house tomorrow there will be a lump in my throat."

Now and then as the years passed we have had the unexpected pleasure of return visits from some of these men.

AFTER THE WAR

- ☐ Arthur continued his work as superintendent of Parks and Recreation and skippered many inter-island trips on the *Mokuola*. As a storyteller he always had a willing audience at the Hawaiʻi Yacht Club.

- ☐ Anne was lovingly known throughout the island as "The Bird Lady" because of programs she gave in the schools to teach students to identify and respect the island birds. Her weekly column on birds was published for

years in the newspaper. She authored four little books: *Hilltop Living in Hawai'i, The Loves of Anne, They Lighted the Friendship Candle, and Sharing Hilltop Living*. She lived out her 88 years at Hilltop.

☐ Peter married Dodie Cameron from Port Townsend, and after the war completed his bachelor's degree at University of Washington. Teaching at Punahou School was his passion and successful career. Their children David, Dan and Diane were raised on the school campus. Later he and Dodie built a home near Hilltop. After retirement he excelled as a Masters competitive swimmer, holding many national and international records.

☐ Jane married Hal Thombs. They and two sons, Tommy and Johnny, made their home in Guam and Hawai'i. In her later years "Auntie Janie" became a beloved frequent floater on cruise ships around the islands. Her 12 scrapbooks of war clippings have recently been found by her son in their attic!

☐ Now 75 years later, "Puna" Peggy (94) and her daughter, Cosette, share Hilltop living. Peggy is proud of her two grandsons and 3 great grandsons. She now takes pleasure in waving to the low flying red Coast Guard helicopter. Sometimes they wave back!

Hilltop House Drive

We respectfully request that readers observe the privacy of our family residence.

Acknowledgements

With pride and gratitude we remember our grandparents Anne "Nani" and Arthur "Skipper" Powlison. They left a legacy of adventure and love for generations to follow.

I thank my cousins for their endless love and support and for carrying on the family traditions with their families.

THANK YOU TO:

Marga Stubblefield for typing.
Joyce Miller for endless hours of scanning.
Toni Withington for days of editing and revision support.
Our Friday discussion group for their encouragement and ideas from day #1.
My mother, Puna Peggy, for her memories and her enthusiasm in this project.
Mark Neal for the map of O'ahu.
Craig and Nancy Smith for making the publishing of this book happen!

PHOTO CREDITS:

59350977R00060

Made in the USA
Charleston, SC
02 August 2016